Roger McGough

Nailing the Shadow

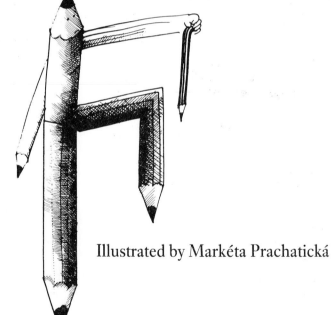

Illustrated by Markéta Prachatická

Viking Kestrel

For Bill Grono and staff at the Western
Australian College of Advanced Education

VIKING KESTREL

Penguin Books Ltd, 27 Wrights Lane, London W8 5TZ (Publishing and Editorial)
and Harmondsworth, Middlesex, England (Distribution and Warehouse)
Viking Penguin Inc., 40 West 23rd Street, New York, New York 10010, U.S.A.
Penguin Books Australia Ltd, Ringwood, Victoria, Australia
Penguin Books Canada Ltd, 2801 John Street, Markham, Ontario, Canada L3R 1B4
Penguin Books (N.Z.) Ltd, 182–190 Wairau Road, Auckland 10, New Zealand

First published 1987

Text copyright © Roger McGough, 1987
Illustrations copyright © Markéta Prachatická, 1987

'Skwerp Eggs' and 'Anteater' first appeared in *The Kingfisher Book of Comic Verse*, published by
    Kingfisher Books
'First Haiku of Spring', 'Prayer to St Grobianus', 'Good Old William' and 'Worry' first
    appeared in *Melting into the Foreground*, published by Viking
'Hundreds and Thousands' first appeared in *Hundreds and Hundreds*, published by Puffin Books

British Library Cataloguing in Publication Data

McGough, Roger
    Nailing the shadow.
    I. Title
    821'.914   PR6063.A219
ISBN 0-670-81801-1

Filmset in Ehrhardt (Linotron 202) by
Rowland Phototypesetting (London) Ltd,
Made and printed in Great Britain by
Butler & Tanner Ltd, Frome and London

Contents

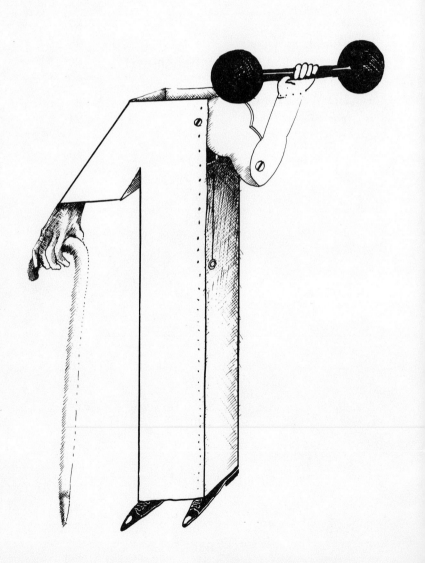

The First

I'd be the first to climb Mount Eiger on a tiger
The first to swim the Channel inside out
The first to run amok in thirty seconds
And train on boiled black pudding, peas and stout.

I'd be the first to win the Ladies' Open Doubles
At Wimbledon, at tennis, on my own
The first to catch a haggis single-handed
And keep it in a cage till fully grown.

I'd be the first to surf Downunder underwater
On the belly of a person-eating shark
Compose a piano fugue for few good reasons
Go on telly then impersonating Bach.

I'd be the first to rollerskate and reach the South Pole
South Polar bears all marvelling at my skill
The first to hang-glide all the way to Venus
And get back quick (because it's all downhill).

I'd be the first to leapfrog over Blackpool Tower
Clear Grand Canyon in one almighty leap.
Dream about the FA Cup at Wembley
Score the winning goal while walking in my sleep.

I'd be the first in all these things
So it's sad to reveal
That maybe now I'm past it
Though they say you're as young as you feel.

Roger McGough (87½)

The Last Straw

'This is the last straw,'
Said teacher. 'The last straw.'

Taking it out, she laid it carefully
On the table next to the others.

'Pencils only, please. And remember,
There is a prize for the winner.'

And so for the next thirty minutes
We all drew straws. (I lost.)

Gazebos

What I find wanting in gazebos
Is their herd instinct.
They either pose woodenly in clearings
Way off the beaten track
Or give us come hither looks
From across a grey smudge of lake.

And always alone. Aloof.
They can't even lay claim
To a collective noun. A posse?
A cluster? A conglomerate?
How they ever manage to reproduce
Is anybody's guess.

Old Wives' Tales (No. 42)

Umpteen years ago
   when I was a teenager
I came out in spots
   (or rather,
spots came out in me).

One day I had
   an ordinary sort of face
and the next,
   as if from outer space
the aliens had landed.

I tried a hundred
   creams and oils
to no avail.
   Those would-be boils,
that gang of bullies
   swaggered around my face
as if they owned it.

So I went to see
   THE OLD WIVES
who told me not to worry.
   'They'll get fed up in time,'
they said, 'and simply go.'
   Now am I pimply? No.

(Instead, there's a network of wrinkles
And hair that comes off with my hat
And other gruesome, yucky things,
But I'll not bother you now with that.)

Love a Duck

I love a duck called Jack
He's my very favourite pet
But last week he took poorly
So I took him to the vet.

The vet said: 'Lad, the news is bad,
Your duck has lost its quack
And there's nowt veterinary science
Can do to bring it back.'

A quackless duck? What thankless luck!
Struck dumb without a word
Rendered mute like a bunged-up flute
My splendid, tongue-tied bird.

All day now on the duvet
He sits and occasionally sighs
Dreaming up a miracle
A faraway look in his eyes.

Like an orphan for his mother
Like a maiden for her lover
Waiting silently is Jack
For the gab to come back

For the gift of tongues that goes . . .

Updown

If you don't feed
      a hungry duck
you might end
      Updown
on your luck

Skwerp Eggs

Have you ever seen
a skwerp?

Ever heard its plain-
tive cry?   (Skwerp! Skwerp!)

Ever tasted a
skwerp egg?

Delicious. Give one
a try.

Fry gently in a
square pan.

(Why not a round one?)
Won't fit.

Cut neatly into
four cubes

Say Grace, then eat
every bit.   (Slurp! Slurp!)

THE MAGIC TENNIS-BALL

(A MYSTERY IN THREE POEMS)

Characters in order of appearance:

> Tom
> Me
> The Gallant Knight
> Lady Elinor
> The Wicked Baron

each   time

Tom   (aged

ten)   and

I   play

ten   nis

he   whacks

the

high   over

the   net

and   right

out   of

the   court

19

NUMBER TWO

In armour bright
A gallant knight
Did journey through the meadow
To free the maiden
That he loved
And kill the Baron dead-o

Fol de rol, Fol de rol,
And kill the Baron dead-o.

On steed, milk-white
All day and night
In sunshine and in shadow
He journeyed long
And sang a song
For he was a handsome lad-o

Fol de rol, Fol de rol,
For he was a handsome lad-o.

Castle in sight
Our gallant knight
Did canter through the meadow
When a tennis-ball
Flew o'er the wall
And hit him on the head-o

Fol de rol, Fol de rol,
And hit him on the head-o.

'Gadzooks,' he cried
The stallion shied
Then galloped off arpeggio
He tried in vain
To hold the rein
But fell into a hedgerow

Fol de rol, Fol de rol,
But fell into a hedgerow.

Fair Elinor
Rolled on the floor
Laughing like a drain. 'Oh,
What a wimple,
He must be simple,
If he wants my hand I'll say no.'

Fol de rol, Fol de rol,
If he wants my hand I'll say no.

The Baron roared
And waved his sword
Staggered helplessly, 'Ho-Ho-Ho.'
Till o'er he keeled
And dropped his shield
And broke his little toe-o

Fol de rol, Fol de rol,
And broke his little toe-o.

No sorrier sight
Than a buckled knight
Jeered at by damsel and foe. So
Cursing them all
He picked up the ball
And gave one almighty throw-o

Fol de rol, Fol de rol,
And gave one almighty throw-o.

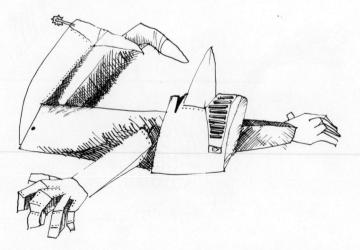

NUMBER THREE

it	lands
back	on
the	court
so	we
can	con
tin	ue
our	game.
Good	Knight.

Portrait of an Earl
(On being awarded an OBE)

In coronet and ermine robe

He poses. The Earlobe.

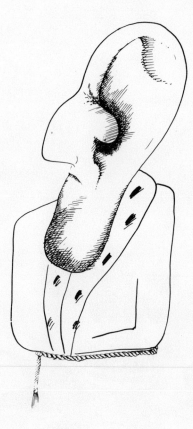

The Town Crier

The Town Crier cried both night and day,
'What knave hath taken my wife away?
I am forsaken, I am undone,
For whom I tolled my bell hath gone.'

Oyez!   Oyez!   Oyez!
Boo hoo Boo hoo Boo hoo.

The Town Crier sat in the darkling square
And blubbered: 'My cupboard, alas, is bare,
No food for my childer, now cold winds blow,
Whither I goest, all is woe.'

Oyez!   Oyez!   Oyez!
Boo hoo Boo hoo Boo hoo.

The Town Crier limped along our street.
'What ails?' I asked. ''Tis my poor feet,
They're killing me,' he sobbed, then sobbèd more.
(So that's, methinks, what a Town Crier's for.)

Merrie England

Though a cold wind
Blows through the barn
The milkmaids sing

As corned-beef hands
Tug at cows
And buckets ring.

Bloat

Meanwhile,
Up at the manor, the squire

Eats a corned-beef sandwich
In front of the fire.

Washes it down with a gallon of porter
Quail by the brace, some brandy and water

A venison's haunch, a lamb's rack
Then wets his whistle with a dry sack.

Pig's belly, umpteen tankards more stout
To give him the benefit of the gout.

Bygones

Never let bygones be bygones.
No sooner are they gone

Than they are back
As Big Ones

Pushing and shoving everyone
Out of the way.

To bygones always say:
        Begone!

Bottoming

Rivulets
of
rain
slide
down
the
windowpane

Like
young
beavers
down
an
icy bank

Bottoming
their
first
winter

Over

Spring   is   overrated

Summer   is   overheated

Autumn   is   overwritten

Winter   is   overthankgod.

First Haiku of Spring

	cuck	oo	cuck	oo	cuck	
oo	cuck	oo	cuck	oo	cuck	oo
	cuck	oo	cuck	oo	cuck	

A Poem with Knickers in It

It's getting Spring.
In Holland Park
Trees brazen it out.

Daffodils in a heap
Around their ankles
Like frilly yellow
     knickers.

Spring Fashion Show

And now April saunters on
Looselimbed and goldenhaired
Wearing a see-through number
Of infinity-blue, appliquéd
With fluffy white clouds.

The designer gets a standing ovation.

(Same dress every year and we still fall for it.)

May

Fields of golden rape,
melting
in the intensity
of their own glowing colour,
slowly
butter the hillsides.

Days

What I admire most about days
Is their immaculate sense of timing.

They appear
inevitably
at first light

Eke
themselves out slowly
over noon

Then edge
surefootedly
toward evening

To bow out
at the very soupçon
of darkness.

Spot on cue, every time.

In Good Hands

Wherever night falls

The earth is always

There to catch it.

Crow

A crow is a crow is a crow
In the bird popularity poll
We are the lowest of the low
But do we care? ( )

While others twitter on and on, or worse
Bang out the same three notes
Of musical morse, we refrain.
If there's 'owt to caw, we caw.

Long since banned from the dawn chorus
We lie in bed until lunchtime
Then leisurely flap down
And bag a few smug worms.

Potter about in the afternoon
Call on friends, or simply bide.
For the night that others hide from
Is the time that we like best.

Nestled in treetops gently swaying
We stretch out to the sky
And hold court with the moon.
Stargazers we. The thinkers.

Looking deep into the heavens
We drift and drift and drift
Up and up into the blueblack
Into the very crowness of the universe.

A crow is a crow is a crow
In the bird popularity poll
We are the lowest of the low
But do we care? ( )

Into the Frying-pan of Eternity

On the floor of the universe
in the furthest unswept corner
where Infinity pauses to get its breath back,
mushrooms grow.

Though edible
they are difficult to pick
because of their size.
In fact, they are so big
that it would take all the people
who ever lived on planet Earth
a million billion zillion light years
to eat even half a one for breakfast.

And just think:
All that butter. Phew.

Anteater

Anteater, Anteater
Where have you been?
Aunt Liz took you walkies
And hasn't been seen.

Nor has Aunt Mary
Aunt Flo or Aunt Di.
Anteater, Anteater
Why the gleam in your eye?

French Version

Tantemanger, Tantemanger
Qu'est-ce que votre jeu?
Tante Claire fait la promenade avec vous
Et poof! Disparue juste comme ça.

Aussi Tante Marie
Tante Flo et Tante Di.
Tantemanger, Tantemanger
Pourquoi la lumière dans l'œil?

$\frac{3}{10}$ See me!

39

In a Baker's Shop Somewhere in Northern France
(After Jean-Paul Sartre)

'A loaf, please,'
said the lady.

'White or brown?'
the baker replied.

'Either, or,'
the lady said,
'I've got my bike outside.'

Author's note: The above poem was composed directly into French and has, I fear, lost something in the translation. Here is the original.

«Dans une boulangerie quelque part à la France du Nord»

«Du pain, s'il vous plaît,»
dit la femme.

«Blanc ou brun?»
répondit le boulanger.

«Ooh, la la, c'est
la même chose,» dit madame,

«en dehors,
il y a ma bicyclette.»

Goldfish
are not
boldfish

They cry
when they
fall over

They tittletat
and chew
the fat

And are glad
when it's
all over.

Gold Fever

Put on my hat and coat
Went down to Hatton Garden
Took a dealer by the throat
Said: 'I beg your pardon,

Got something you want to buy
Wink wink, no questions asked
Make an offer, make it high
I want money, want it fast.'

He took it, he weighed it
Smiled, nodded his head
Then gave me forty quid
For a goldfish, slightly dead.

Old Wives' Tales (No. 18)

When I was a child
I caught measles. Then
I caught mumps. After that
I caught tonsillitis. A month later
I caught influenza. As soon as I was better
I caught pneumonia. So my mother took me to see
THE OLD WIVES
Who advised dipping my fingers
In butter every morning.
So I did. And since then
I have not caught a thing.

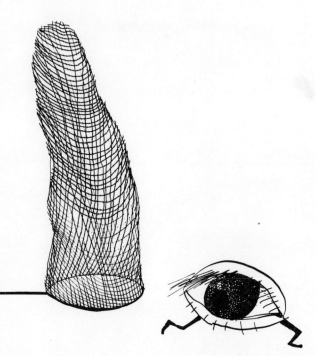

The Cackle

Cut the cackle
and get the gist

heat the kettle
and wet the wrist

raise the hackle
and cock the snook

shake the rattle
and sling the hook

trim the tackle
and nook the cranny

lick the pickle
and tickle your granny.

Three Cock-a-snooks

(i)   'The major here bagged a leopard
Two baboons and a giraffe,
Whereas I just about managed
To cock a snook.'

(ii)   'An if oi catch ee playin
In moi cornflake fields again,'
Said the ruddy-voiced farmer
To the ragamuffins,
'You'll really cock a snook.'

(iii)   'And no daughter of mine
Is going to marry
A commonorgarden cockasnook
I don't care how much
His mercedes benz.'

Two Beck and Call Poems

(i)   You know where we live
It's not far at all
Any time you're passing
Feel free to beck and call.

(ii) 'Beck and call'
Beckoned the Beck and Caller,
So we all becked and called
(It's no life for an underling*).

*Guess how often underlings
Wash their little underthings?

47

P's and Q's

I puite often confuse

My quees and my poos.

Peas and Cues

There's a little shop in Kew
Selling multicoloured peas
I use some in my stews
The remaining few I freeze

A chopstick for a cue
Then down upon my knees
Play snooker when I choose
And pot the peas with ease.

ough

Sophie Clough
went to Slough.

Hough?

Chough-chough.

Good Old William

'I concur
With everything you say,'
Smiled William.

'Oh yes,
I concur with that,
I agree.'

'If that's the general feeling
You can count on me.
Can't say fairer.'

Good old
William, the Concurrer.

Downhill Racer

Down
        the
            snow
                white
            page
        we
slide.
    From
            side
                to
                    side
                we
            glide.
            Pass
                obstacles
                        with
                            ease.
                        Words
                    on
                skis.
        Look out.
                Here
            comes
        a
    poem
        in
            a
                hurry!

Uphill Climb

Wheeeeee
Three
Two
One
go.
another
have
to
top
the
to
back

way

the

all

climb

the

is

part

boring

only

The

Clerihew

Jane Austen

Got lost in

Stoke-on-Trent

Moral: She shouldn't have went.

An Acrostic

A favourite literary devi
Ce is the one whe
Re the first letter
Of each line spell
S out the subject the poe
T wishes to write about.
I must admit, I
Can't see the point myself.

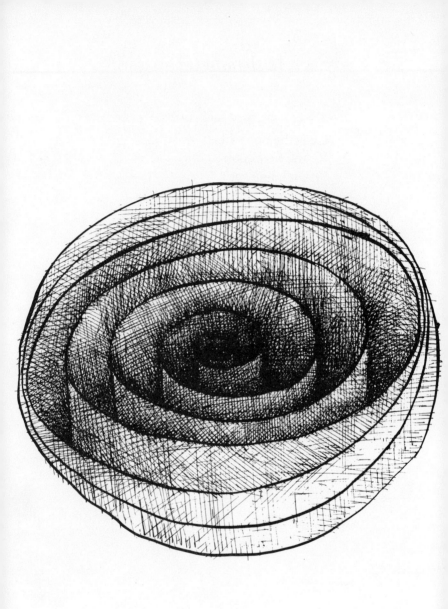

Poor Old Ox
(A Boustrophedon*)

must so plough oxen the As
this be read As a pinball
rink tilted its down runs
and away with your money
words few these wind so
Wrestler thrown across the ring
Wool rope to rope from
unravelling Coil unwinding
Staircase skeltering Helter
spiralling Tiring Boring
furrowing Brow
Field unzipping
ox old Poor

*A Greek word meaning 'as the ox turns in ploughing'. Read this
from right to left, then head back in the opposite direction.

Riddle

My first is in barrow but not in wheel
My second imagined but not unreal
My third is in bird but not in nest
My fourth wears undies but never a vest
My fifth is in lemons but not in squeezes
My sixth is in ice and thrice in sneezes
My whole is something that pleases and teases.

Answer: Riddle

Another Riddle

Though giving pleasure to many
I am no more than a passing fancy,

A bagatelle. Am looked down upon
by my peers for my sense of fun.

Jealous introverts, they think me flippant
Empty-headed I may be, but not irreverent.

I glister, am all show, all style
Here is the key, come inside: I'll make you smile.

Answer: Another riddle

Intermezzo

Beethoven Bartók Bizet and Bruckner
Delius Debussy Mozart and Mahler
Satie Scarlatti Stravinsky and Wagner
Tchaikovsky Vaughan Williams Varèse and Weber

Sibelius Shostakovitch Schubert and Schumann
Dvořák and Fauré Schoenberg and Chopin
Prokofiev Grieg Walton Stockhausen
Offenbach Handel Haydn and Mendelssohn

Elgar Ravel Rachmaninov Rossini
Berlioz Britten Purcell Paganini
Liszt Monteverdi Holst and Vivaldi
Brahms J. S. Bach Rimsky-Korsakov Verdi

Beatles and Beach Boys Bowie and Wham!
Dylan Deep Purple Rod Stewart Steeleye Span
Springsteen Stevie Wonder Sting Elton John
Rolling Stones Elvis The Who Duran Duran.

The Crazy Drummer

Because
he whipped up a storm
in a band
on a ship

We all had to
abandon ship.

*I've no idea. Better ask an overling.

On the Beach

FIRST LADY: Help, my husband is drowning!

CHORUS OF BATHERS: Nice day for it.

SECOND LADY: Help, my husband, who is terribly rich, is drowning!

CHORUS OF BATHERS: Tell him to hold on, we're coming.

Moral: (Not very.)

Seascouts

Yesterday
while walking saw
30 seascouts
on the shore.
They were joined
by 40 more.
Alas! I thought
does this mean
WAR?

The Last TV Commercial

(For Adrian Henri)

Girls,
When he takes you in his arms
For that final, four-minute kiss,
You need an extra-special lipstick.

For a kiss he'll remember always
Be sure you're wearing:
Apocolipstick

Apocolipstick
Just one of *Relvon's*
Exciting new range of
Holocosmetics.

Prayer to Saint Grobianus

(The patron saint of coarse people)

Intercede for us dear saint we beseech thee
  we fuzzdutties and cullions
  dunderwhelps and trollybags
  lobcocks and loobies.

On our behalf seek divine forgiveness for
  we puzzlepates and pigsconces
  ninnyhammers and humgruffins
  gossoons and clapperdudgeons.

Have pity on we poor wretched sinners
  we blatherskites and lopdoodles
  lickspiggots and clinchpoops
  quibberdicks and quakebuttocks.

Free us from the sorrows of this world
and grant eternal happiness in the next
  we snollygosters and gundyguts
  gongoozlers and groutheads
  ploots, quoobs, lurds and swillbellies.

As it was in the beginning, is now, and ever shall be,
world without end. OK?

The Power of Prayer

When the mugger mugs
Or the bully pounces
Pray to St Peter
(Patron Saint of Bouncers)

Poem for a Lady Wrestler

There be none of Beauty's daughters
    who can wrestle like thee
And like depth-charges on the waters
    is thy sweet voice to me.

Thy muscles are like tender alps
    with strength beyond compare
Of all the Ladies of the Rings
    there is none so fair.

Thy half-nelsons and thy head-locks
    thy slammings to the floor
are bliss. But in bedsocks
    and pyjamas I love thee even more.

Toupee

He wears dead hair on his head.
A mat, handwoven from tresses
Shorn from Tuscan nuns.

He thinks he looks
Ten years younger
But it's twenty years too late

For the man with half a badger
Dyed ginger
And glued to his pate.

Elephant Joke

(A Just So Story)

Once upon a time, on the banks of the River Indus,
south of Lahore, two elephants
were having a lazy game of trunk-wrestling.
In between bouts, one said:
'Because you are my friend, I will tell
you a secret: I don't like Irish jokes.'

The other, who was indeed his friend,
begged him to explain.

'Quite simply, because they belittle
and demean the Irish.'

His friend nodded in agreement,
ruminated for a short while, and then asked:
'But what about rhinoceros jokes?'
'Ah, but that's different,' said the first elephant,
'rhinoceros jokes are funny.'

'Just so,' agreed his friend.
And the two pakiderms fell about,
snortling with unbridled laughter.

Me and My Ilk

Me and my ilk
Are as brave as silk
As cagey as lions in a zoo

Me and my ilk
Are as handsome as milk
(The antithesis of you).

Me and My Shadow

Me and my sha – dow
Went out for a drink last night.
Me and my sha – dow
Came home just a li – ttle tight

    At twelve o'clock
    We reached the flat
    Un – locked the door
    Co – llapsed on the mat

Then su – dden – ly no – ticed
Ly – ing in the spi – nning hall
The sha – dow I lay with
Clear – ly was – n't mine at all

So who's got my sha – dow
Will the one who's ta – ken it
Please send my sha – dow
Back because this one is several sizes too big and doesn't fit

Uncle Roger

I am distinctly
ununclely.
I forget birthdays
and give Xmas presents
only when cornered.
(Money, of course, and too little.)

I am regrettably
ununclish.
Too thin to be jolly,
I can never remember
jokes or riddles.
Even fluff
my own poems.

My nephews and nieces
as far as I know
disuncled
me some time ago.
Better uncleless
than my brand of petty
uncleness.

Fame

The best thing
about being famous

is when you walk
down the street

and people turn round
to look at you

and bump into things.

The Gasman

Why do people call you the Gasman?

Because I go round reading metres.

A Mersey Christmas

De rain
De snows
De cold in
De nose
De girls
De boys
De expensive toys
De shops all packed
De old girl whacked
De men on de dole
De old King Cole
De fairy lights
De silent nights
De Xmas cheer
De end of de year
De glowing ember
December.

Rubbery Chicken

(In a Chinese restaurant in Liverpool)

'Aye, Waiter – over 'ere!

This chicken tastes like rubber
The pork's just cobs of fat
The noodles are all tangled
And the gravy smells of cat.

The onions are hard as breadboards
The beansprouts are covered in fur
It says mushrooms on the menu
But there's hardly any there.

The crispy ducks are like toenails
And there's dandruff in the rice
And muddy footprints round the plate
Made by bluddy mice.

Chow mein? Never again!
The thought of it makes me ill.
So what, if I did eat the lot?
(Could you knock a few bob off the bill?)'

US Flies in Hamburgers*

If you go down the High Street today
You'll be sure of a big surprise
When you order your favourite burger
With a milkshake and regular fries.

For the secret is out
I tell you no lies
They've stopped using beef
In favour of FLIES.

FLIES, FLIES, big juicy FLIES,
FLIES as American as apple pies.

Horseflies, from Texas, as big as your thumb
Are sautéed with onions and served in a bun.

Free-range bluebottles, carefully rinsed
Are smothered in garlic, and painlessly minced.

Black-eyed bees with stings intact
Add a zesty zing, and that's a fact.

Colorado beetles, ants from Kentucky,
Rhode Island roaches, and if you're unlucky

Baltimore bedbugs (and even horrider)
Leeches as squashy as peaches from Florida.

FLIES, FLIES, big juicy FLIES,
FLIES as American as mom's apple pies.

It's lovely down in MacDingles today
But if you don't fancy flies
Better I'd say to keep well away
Stay home and eat Birds' Eyes.

*Newspaper headline referring to hamburgers being airlifted to
feed homesick US marines.

Mr Take Away

They call me Mr Take Away
I carry out throughout the land
While others eat home-cooking
In some long queue I stand

Mondays it's fish and chips
Tuesdays chicken chow mein
Wednesdays it's pizza
Thursdays chips again

Fridays Kentucky fried
Saturdays a doner
On Sundays I bike
To the Spud-I-Don't-Like
(It's no good being a loner).

Hide and Seek

When I played as a kid

How I longed to be caught

But whenever I hid

Nobody sought.

Tumble Down

In Turvy Town
On Tumble Down
Great Architects conspire

The Hollow men
Shake hands and then
Walk into the fire

The Queen of Straw
Does jiggle more
As the flames leap higher

Ring-a-ring
The children sing
All in a cage of briar

Ashoo Ashoo
We are all tumbled down

Ashoo Ashoo
We are all tumbled down

Hundreds and Thousands

The sound of hounds
on red sand thundering

Hundreds and thousands
of mouths glistening

The blood quickening
Thunder and lightning

The hunted in dread
of the hundreds running

The sound of thunder
A white moon reddening

Thousands of mad hounds
on red sand marauding

Thundering onwards
in hundreds and thundreds

Thundreds and thundreds
Thundering   Thundering

The Poltergeese

The poltergeese
  their mischief done
are heading north
  to miss the sun.

Leaving behind
  a trail of woe
havoc reeks
  where e'er they go.

Mad harbingers
  of disrepair
stopped
  clock, broken chair.

Coven flying
  overhead
can curdle milk
  move the bed.

Fretful curtain
  creaking stair
doorbell rings n-
  nobody there.

Wanting a reason
  you look to the sky
are given a V-sign
  in reply.

Depressed?

When you're

depressed

deep rest

is best.

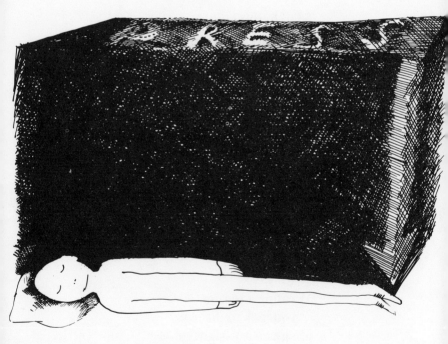

Worry

Where would we be without worry?
It helps keep the brain occupied
DOING doesn't take your mind off things
I've tried.

Worry is God's gift to the nervous
Best if kept bottled inside.
I once knew a man who couldn't care less.
He died.

The Ghost Narrator

Each night the Ghost Narrator
With our secrets to share
Greets an audience of billions
Tuned in somewhere out there.

At the end of every little scene
Just before the ads
He steps out and moralizes
To the celestial mums and dads.

One by one unwittingly
We play the starring role
While he creates suspense
As to the outcome of the soul.

And when our episode is over
And all is pain and sorrow
He's there at the deathbed, smiling:
'Goodnight. Same time tomorrow.'

Ten Questions I'd Rather Not Answer

    i) Why did they nail her shadow to the ground?

   ii) Has the mirror seen the last of me?

  iii) Out there, are they whispering, or shouting quietly?

  iv) If I hit the headlines, will they hit me back?

   v) My first memory: in my cot playing with a death rattle?

  vi) Why is the sixth one always so difficult?

 vii) Words left unsaid, are they sad, do they wither away?

viii) Can the darkness be pacified?

  ix) Where do my hands finish?

   x) Why is my mouth screaming?

Let me explain...

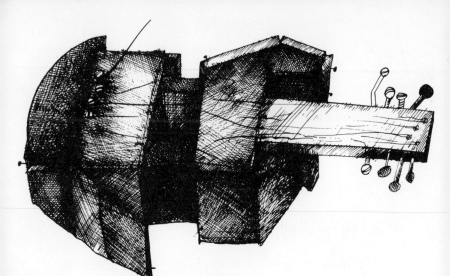

Blackest of Blues

(A song)

I was born in Dread County
Wrong side of the track
Raised by an Apache
In an old chicken shack
Never knew who my pa was
Ma she died young
I ain't got no money
But I got a song.

My baby she left me
For a slick city dude
Got eight or nine children
And I can't buy 'em food
The roof is a-leakin
The rain starts to fall
If you've had some troubles
Boy, I got 'em all.

Old Shep got run over
Just the other day
Pigs got pneumonia
Chickens won't lay
There's rats in the bedroom
Dead skunk in the well
Apache in the cupboard
Is starting to smell.

Tried to get drafted
Cos I needed the pay
But they called off the war
The very next day
So I burned down the Courthouse
To look at the flame
Got a burning ambition
I might do it again.

Got a shelf full of magazines
But I can't read
Got a mouthful of bad teeth
And they're startin to bleed
Shot my foot off while huntin
Good job I had two
Got the blackest of blues
Gonna lay 'em on you.

My kids have all left me
As far as I know
Wind is a-howlin
It's startin to snow
The only fire I got
Is the fire in the booze
I'm one of life's losers
All I got is the blues.

Feller's just called
Says there's oil on my land
My troubles are over
Gonna be a rich man
Now a rattlesnake's bit me
As I'm puttin on my shoe(s)
Ain't no happy ending
To this blackest of blues.

Chorus:
I sure knows what the blues are
I sure knows what the blues are
I sure knows what the blues are
I got the Blackest of Blues.

All's Well That Ends

Peter was awake as soon as daylight sidled into his
bedroom. Saturday at last. He jumped out of bed and
flung open the curtains. Thank goodness, he thought,
not a cloud in the sky. As he gazed out of the window, he
wondered about the day ahead. Would his school team
win the county cricket trophy? *(No.)* Would he score his
first century? *(No, l.b.w. second ball.)* Would
Helen be at the party in the evening? *(Yes)* Would she
let him dance with her, walk her home and kiss her? *(No,
she'd spend all night smooching and snogging with
O'Leary.)* Would the police discover Grandma's body
behind the woodshed? *(Yes, on Monday.)* And if so,
would they think it was an accident? *(No, sorry.)* Or
suicide? *(Hardly.)* Would he be incarcerated? *(What's
that?)* Put in prison *(Yes.)*

But during his time inside, wouldn't he determine to
make amends, study hard and gain early parole?
Wouldn't he find a steady job and settle down? One day
meet a decent girl and raise a family? Eventually,
wouldn't he own a national chain of DIY supermarkets,
give money to charity, become a model citizen respected
and loved by the whole community?
Say yes *(No.)*
But surely all's well that ends? *(Well . . . . . .*

Index of First Lines

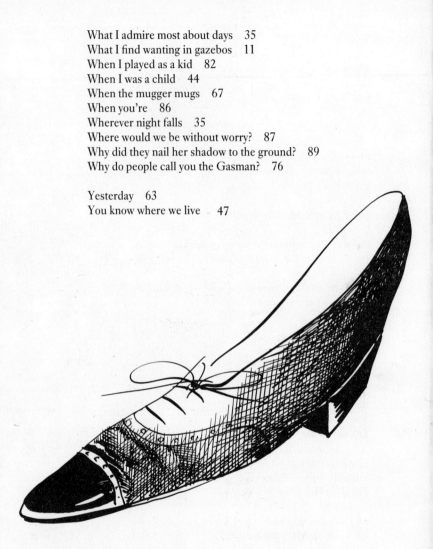